THESE

COLORS

DON'T

run

eytys   **robert lindholm**   **martina almquist**

THESE COLORS DON'T RUN

A New York Love Story

Populist winds are knocking at the doors of Western society, urging the undereducated and underserved to think that diversity and inclusion are to blame for their woes. Our political establishments are not chasing what is morally right, but trying to chase the tides of the loudest, most angered voters, no matter what their battle cry. We had taken two steps forward and seem to be running to hit three steps backward in record time – all the headway we have made as a collective society to include and live in harmony with all ethnicities, religions, sexual orientations, and genders, is under attack, mostly because as a race we fear the unknown or the unfamiliar.

With this book, we wanted to make an ode to the New York Dream – which is the contemporary iteration of the American Dream for the interconnected, global, digital nationality of youth. New York is a symbol for how the diversity experiment has and can continue to yield positive results and that fostering exchange can electrify a city with ideas, art, creativity, and, at the end of the day, life.

New York has always been the physical home of artists, of ambitious youth running away from a boring hometown or overbearing parents or never-there parents, of immigrants looking for an opportunity. But it's also the proverbial home for those that feel connected to the spirit of New York from around the world, who may only know the city through Martin Scorcese movies or Basquiat and Andy Warhol, or any of the other millions of love letters and postcards written about this exponentially reverberating place. The collective idea of New York makes it our global shared city.

♡ Eytys

The
(163rd st) Bronx, NY

TRUMP

OUTSIDER MOGUL CA
STUNNING CLINTON I

ork Times

NOVEMBER 9, 2016

Late Edition

Today, cloudy, showers midday, high
58. Tonight, stray evening showers,
clouds breaking late, crode low t
Tomorrow, sunshine, high e
late, busy, cop. son la ge f

RIUMPHS

ES THE PRESIDENCY,
BATTLEGROUND STATES

WORKING CLASS SPEAK

br All tes Giv
St ging Rebuke to
D mocratic P ty

By PATRICK HEAL
and JONATHAN MAR N

Donald John T mp w
elected the 45th pre ent of th
United S es on sday in
stunning ulmination f an explo
sive bu s zing camp
that clouds ders ness am
the institution and long-hel
ideals of American democracy.
The surprise outcome, defying
late polls that showed Hillar
Clinton with a modest but persist
ed c reated convinced
th untry

PAWN SHOP

JEWELRY

Anytime

WHAT IS YOUR BEST ADVICE TO TRUMP?

Chill out

ANARCHIST CHIC

by Kaitlin Phillips

The dating pool is never larger, and never so clear a blue, as when you're young and living in a city. At your disposal? Famous musicians who can't sleep, pathological liars, skaters who layer long sleeve shorts under short sleeve shirts, genius dropouts, poets on speed, domestic terrorists, bad boy alcoholics, good-looking and sullen baristas, angry "outsider artists," even boomer artists, and those people who go to parties just to hand out their zines – none of these are gendered professions, in fact all of these people are studied nonprofessionals. They required no education to get where they are, or too much education. If you're in luck they're sleeping on a ratty couch, or a crawlspace, or way out at the end of the earth, in a neighborhood with sidewalks overrun with weeds, eerily empty at sunup, where you can walk in the middle of the street and make eye contact with hobos.

If you're in New York – and if you aren't that's fine because you will be eventually – you can find any type of person you want. What you're going to want to do, in 2018, is find an anarchist or a marxist with overflowing shelves, someone with politics, even if they don't go in for bumperstickers. They're going to teach you how to shoplift, and show you videos of the battle in Seattle. And they're going to take you to some protests, maybe let you walk in the black bloc, do tacky stuff like join the drum circle. You can learn a lot about adrenaline by watching people throw trash cans at cars.

Protests are the new shopping mall, that's where you can see what everyone's wearing. Malls were built for people to spend money. Malls were coopted by teens, who didn't go to the mall to spend money, they went to smoke, and steal things, and pout publicly if they should so choose. If you want to go hang out with no purpose, but maybe make enough eye contact to secure a phone number – or maybe you just need to stretch your legs, and want to keep your headphones in. That's what the protest is for now. You can paint a sign, and leave it in the street as litter, or art, if someone picks it up and takes it home. It's a roving food court, you can grab a hotdog from the guy at the corner with his cart. Where else do you get to yell at a passersby while you're shopping / bombs are dropping.

The point is not what you're doing or who you're with, as long as you met them outside and they're not a republican. Don't trust anyone who doesn't take long walks. Because then they're missing the shitty Laundromat with peeling wallpaper run by a Korean woman who watches Law and Order SVU on her iPad all day. And the 24-hour Indian buffet that plays Bollywood films on a loop. (Go literally everywhere that's open 24 hours, from spas to delis, run them like a trap line, sampling the goods and surveying the locals.) Those midnight horror movies – sometimes, if the cinema is empty enough like in Kipps Bay, you can see the rats running between the seats. Do wait until last call at the club, stumbling out with whoever else made it to 4:15, and dragging them to get a greasy slice. Go to the French bistros off Houston where the French models go to drink coffee and watch their dates eat steaks. Always order the fries, they're never more than $8. Crash a house party if you see people going in off the street, especially those where they keep the Christmas lights taped up on the walls all year round. Go to The Cock, the gay bar in New York – or any nightlife institution that you don't know when they're gonna fail. Any business on its last legs, like a bakery that only makes marzipan, that's where you want to be seen, that's where you're going to find people with free time to hang out with you. Trust those boys who play basketball in the park, but no one who goes to Equinox. Take the subway in every direction, to the end of the line. There are beaches there. Keep those people around who can talk themselves into anything, past any bouncer.

And, since you're not at the mall, don't buy anything. Suss up literally everything you can get for free. Drink the beers at openings, eat the bread baskets. And always ask someone else for a light – it's an excuse to talk to smokers, the most jaded people in New York. As long as you make some strangers your people, and they skip work to bum around the city with you, then you're fine. You know you've made it.

Kaitlin Phillips is a writer in New York, where she went to boarding school and college. She lives on the Upper East Side with her boyfriend, but spends all her time at a French bistro on 1st and 1st.

揚記麵廠
TON SPECIALIST INC.
AYETTE ST. NEW YORK, N.Y. 10013
1800-234-0894 FAX:212-219-2903

WHERE DID YOU GROW UP?

New York,

AT IS YOUR FAVOURITE THING ABOUT NYC?

diversity of people & culture.

Reeccarnete / Come

its iconic, Alot of opportuniti
and' interesting people.

WHAT IS YOUR FAVOURITE THING ABOUT NYC?

It's raw, gritty, and ruthless, yet so beautiful.

THE SPECTRUM BECAME THE DREAMHOUSE

by Michael J. Bullock

> "A dream you dream alone is only a dream, A dream you dream together is reality."
>
> -Yoko Ono

A plain white tote bag posted on Instagram by the DJ and composer A Village Raid makes a timely-curious pronouncement "GENDER IS A SPECTRUM/SPECTRUM IS NOW THE DREAMHOUSE." The peculiar phrase in the digital artifact means nothing to most people, but to the current batch of New York City's gender fluid, queer creative youth the words cheekily sum up the trajectory of the most unlikely and influential night clubs of this decade. In the past, the legendary clubs of New York have always been key in reflecting and expanding the possibilities of city life. They have been important social engines, places where freedom and experimentation were lived out: art, performance, fashion, personality, music, dancing, drugs and sex all simmered together. Style was invented. Values solidified. Communities formed. The allure and promise of these iconic institutions sent signals out into the greater world through magazines like *Interview* and *PAPER* calling outcast teenagers to leave their small towns and come join a new family; a nightlife culture that in most regards had inverse values to puritanical suburban society. In these special places diversity was celebrated, hedonism was a shared achievement, ideas were exchanged and developed and culture mutated and evolved in real time on the dance floor as the talented minds and beautiful bodies of each era literally came together, synthesized, satisfied and supportive of each other. Generations grew up together. These magic places had a transformative effect on their participants leaving a lasting impact on the greater city and sometimes society at large.

In the storied clubs where the stars aligned with basic architecture, ordinary dive bars, churches and warehouses became alternative fantasy worlds. The places that achieved this are celebrated often: CBGB's, THE MUDD CLUB, MAX's KANSAS CITY, STUDIO 54, PARADISE GARAGE, AREA, LIMELIGHT and TUNNEL. But in the early aughts evil Giuliani and his silly Cabaret Licenses had a death grip on this radiant world. Mayor Bloomberg doubled down on this, helping to further transform the artist city into a billionaire's paradise. Putting nightlife entrepreneurs on the run and rushing almost all of what made going out in the city great. Corporate clubs thrived, bankers and bottle service proliferated and the city ran on nostalgic fumes of its former glory. It looked as if the possibility of the club as a prototype of utopia was a thing of the past. An experience that could only be accessed through documentaries that make you wish you had been born forty years earlier. By 2010, the "Sex in the City" clones had won. Manhattan had become a sanitized, million-dollar apartment, asset-driven, luxury island. But while the wealth rusted Manhattan's creativity, the raw outer limits of Brooklyn began to flourish – illegal clubs slipped under the radar, most disappeared as quickly as they began, except for one: The Spectrum.

This is how a typical weekend would go: At 3 AM on a Saturday night that was nowhere close to ending, the next stop would have to be Montrose Ave, an unassuming street in the Puerto Rican section of Williamsburg. Looking at a group of quiet row houses, you wonder, is it happening tonight? As you try to remember which door would lead you to The Spectrum. When you choose right, your night begins. A friendly security guard with the silhouette of a scorpion shaved into the hair on the back of his head ushers you off the street into a long peach-colored hallway. Here you were greeted by a floor-to-ceiling message scrolled across the wall in purple spray paint. It read: "Thank you for helping us maintain a safe queer community space." These grateful words gently remind you that what you're about to experience is not just any nightclub, The Spectrum was the product of an ethos deeply rooted in queer politics. It told you: if you found The Spectrum, you were a part of The Spectrum. It's wasn't VIP. Doors were open to all, but being there meant that you were a member of a self-selecting family made up of disenfranchised members of society, lost boys and girls of every kind, queer, trans, gay-orphans, artists, performers, gypsies, freaks, punks and hedonists. Once though the narrow, dark hallway, you came upon an expansive mirrored dance floor. This is what you came for: a sea of sweaty revelers in various states of undress, dancing in a trance, engaged in a celebration of each others' music and art, minds and bodies.

The Spectrum might be described as a nightlife co-op where every quest contributed their part in order to make it happen. While many people may have thought of it as an after-hours, it's actually 24-hours-a-day of queer action. Its structure was unique: the decadence of the night was built upon the creative productivity that happened in the space during the day. In 2011, the performance artist, Gage of the Boone found the live/work location on Craigslist, "I wanted a place to live, make art and rehearse, I was trying to figure out how I could live in an alternative way. I had always wanted a queer community space." Gage explains. Two of his closest friends helped to round out his vision, his roommate, artist Raúl De Nieves and Danny Taylor aka A Village Raid who was the resident DJ and music curator.

In the Instagram era where nightlife is about projecting your good time, The Spectrum benefited from being the last stop of the night, you arrived after all your personal PR work was finished and you were ready to get messy. Taylor explains, "The environment forced people to let go no matter what they were wearing because once inside your look just didn't last long, you would have to just take it all off. I saw some of the most precious people strip down and just get on with it. People's facades had a way of dissolving inside The Spectrum."

From it's humble starting point, The Spectrum grew organically into an international cultural hub presenting cutting-edge music and performance art and becoming a hotbed for emerging talent. In it's short run, many of the participants came into their own becoming widely recognized, artist and fashion designers such as Telfar, Hood By Air, DIS, Marie Karlberg, Stewart Uoo, Jacolby Satterwhite, Juliana Huxtable, Boychild, DeSe and musically Lafawndah, Total Freedom, Arca, Carrie Nation, Michael Magnan, Zebra Katz, Mykki Blanco, Banjee Report and House of Ladosha. "These people have been in our lives for a long time. It's awesome to be able to celebrate your friends. They stuck with their beliefs and made it possible – most of the people that I see that are really successful, it's because they have stuck together and built a community, it's not just a single person being like I'm awesome! I'm Picasso! It's like Picasso is now a group of people!" exclaims De Nieves.

But sadly, on New Year's Eve, 2016, The Spectrum threw its last party, becoming the latest casualty of New York's rapid-fire real-estate market. This should have been the end of the story, a five-year run already put it in lineage of the legends (AREA also lasted 5 years) but the need the space had identified and filled was too great. The Spectrum may have been gone but the community that had grown around it was thriving and still needed it's clubhouse. The trio Gage, Danny and Raul were not to be stopped. In 2017, with bravery and passion they signed the lease on a space in Bay Ridge, Queens that is three times the size of the original Spectrum. The interior was an exercise in extreme decorating, an Ecuadorian banquet hall through the filter of a '90s J.Lo music video (the owner is a set designer). In it's first year there has been an expansion of the programming, and the new multilevel space includes artist studios, bigger spaces for rehearsal, and photography, and now there's monthly family dinners, Aikido and self defense kickboxing classes, a gay-but-all-inclusive sex party titled BANQUET, an all-female sex party titled BUFFET, and a poetry reading series titled NIGHT FLIGHT TO VENUS. It hosts screenings of films where emerging composers rescore classic movies like "Cruising" or "The Shining," a bi-monthly outpost of a Berlin-based techno fetish party named UNTER, along with the space's signature celebrations NIGHTS OF THE TEMPLAR and OVER THE RAINBOW.

There is a beautiful moment that happens every time I'm at The Spectrum that defines how important the place is to New York. At some point in the evening I'll meet a queer boy or girl, about 20 years old, that's just moved to the city who will ask in awe, "What is this place and how does it exist?" You can see the revelation of new possibilities in their expression. In that instant their realizing the oppressive economics of the city don't need to own their life, that persuing their own art might be a possibility, that an underground world exists that could support them. Some of New York's greatest art and LGBTQ organizations started out grassroots out of necessity: The New Museum, PS1 (now MOMA PS1), Callen Lord, and The Center (The Lesbian, Gay, Bisexual & Transgender Community Center). The DREAMHOUSE is in an important linage of nightlife, activism, and art institutions and combines the three types of activity into a unique but fluid program that is a wonderful and necessary evolution of queer urban life. But even after so much acclaim, the community center still operates as an independent, illegal night club with the stress of the enormous rent on the backs of it's founders. My hope for the DREAMHOUSE is that it can become a permanent part of New York City's cultural landscape. That just like the other institutions mentioned, it is recognized by the local government as an essential part of the city's vitality and they find a way to fund it without ruining it's experimental, free spirit. Right now, creating and maintaining this club unsupported is a generous act of political activism. Gage sums it up "I often have to remind myself that it is my radical duty, my radical artwork, and it's a labor of love."

Michael J. Bullock is a writer, journalist and publisher that lives in Bedford–Stuyvesant, Brooklyn. He started his career in publishing at the grandfather of the modern independent magazine index (from 2000–2004) and went on to set up BUTT (the revolutionary dutch homosexual magazine) in America, becoming it's US publisher (2003–2011). Currently he is the American features editor for the contemporary interiors magazine Apartamento, a regular contributor to the architecture and design title PIN–UP, and works on the publishing side of Fantastic Man, The Gentlewoman, and PIN–UP. In 2013, Karma Books published his novella Roman Catholic Jacuzzi.

恆星傳訊

星傳訊

SPRINKLER
FIRE DEPT.
CONNECTION

AUTOMATIC SPRINKLER
SHUT OFF VALVE
FEET
OSITE THIS SIGN

working hard + playing harder

growing up in East NY. My entire family was
in. It's definitely where I found my love of
writing and Art. (Adolescent years)
As an Adult, still Brooklyn. I live here w/
of my life and I am going to
The love of my city and space.
in the

WHAT IS YOUR FAVOURITE THING ABOUT NY

I CAN DO WHATEVER I WANT HERE. IF I WANT TO WAKE UP TOMORROW + BE SOMEONE COMPLETELY DIFFERENT, I CAN ALSO GOOD MUSIC.

WHAT IS YOUR FAVOURITE THING ABOUT NYC?
bodegas

Rogers Av

moved 房 back to NY

EDWARD HOPPER'S "AUTOMAT" AND THE LONELY POSSIBILITIES OF NEW YORK

by Cody Delistraty

"Automat," a 1927 painting by Edward Hopper, is peculiar in that the subject – a young, well-dressed woman sitting inside an automat at a stone table with a cup of coffee – appears lonely and sad, and yet the picture itself is not sad.

A turn-of-the-century invention in which basic food and drinks are served out of vending machines (like an even more frictionless Pret A Manger), an automat is a place in which there might be no human interaction at all. It is, in other words, exactly the kind of place you'd go if you wanted to be left alone. There are many places in New York City like this, where the painting is most likely set. At the time of painting it Hopper was in his mid-forties, living on Washington Square Park in Manhattan with his wife, Josephine, who modeled for the picture. And yet, while it would make sense to go somewhere lonesome if you wanted to be alone, an automat is also exactly the kind of place you might end up going even if you desperately don't want to be alone.

That's the brutal thing about loneliness and the grandness and anonymity of New York City: it makes you all the more lonely so that even when you desire the company of others, you might find that you've been alone for long enough that you're no longer even sure how to broach socializing, how to enter into a bar and meet people, how to strike up a conversation on the street. Loneliness is exponential – the longer you stay lonely the harder it is to break from it.

There is, without a doubt, an increasing corporate dullness to New York City. Since its crime rate fell drastically in the mid-1990s (when the then-mayor Rudy Giuliani applied the "broken window" theory in which all minor infractions were consistently and more severely punished by police) and its financial sector significantly expanded, driving up rents and hence driving out many lifelong New Yorkers, many believed that the spirit of the city had been lost.

Indeed, no longer is Greenwich Village a derelict place, perfect for the creativity of Jean-Michel Basquiat or Andy Warhol. No longer is Harlem the bastion of jazz and so much progressive art. No longer can a young enterprising spirit move to the city with a few dollars in her pocket and feasibly try to make it big.

And yet, New York still affords one the power to be alone, to set oneself adrift in a way that can be done in few other places. The American obsession with the individual, with the self-made experience comes to a head in New York, and, with it, all of the utter possibility inherent in a place as large and varied and chalked full of opportunities.

In "Automat," the bright lights, the unremarkable furniture, the dullness of the space might have been a relief to the young woman with her coffee. Perhaps here she was able to more easily give into her sadness, to reckon with her feelings. She does not seem to feel entirely at home in this painting, just as none of Hopper's lonely characters are ever at that kind of ease. No, they are in motel rooms and diners and service stations. But here, in the automat, the picture is not sad. It is a picture that invites us to emphasize, that is made powerful by the potency of its melancholy. Possibility lies in front of her. And, just as much as we might miss the New York of old, there is no reason to be particularly sad for it. The potential of the space remains.

Cody Delistraty is a writer and critic who lives in Paris. For many years, he lived in the Nolita neighborhood of New York while he attended N.Y.U. Later, after returning to New York from his graduate studies at Oxford, he lived in the East Village, on the fringe of Alphabet City.

WHAT IS YOUR BEST ADVICE TO TRUMP?

 Talk less, listen more.

these colours don't run

PHOTOGRAPHY	Robert Lindholm
STYLING	Martina Almquist
CASTING DIRECTOR	Trevor Swain
EDITOR	Caroline Gaimari
TEXTS	Cody Delistraty
	Kaitlin Phillips
	Michael J. Bullock
MODELS	Ace
	Eddy LeRoy Jr.
	Isabella Enrico
	Isaiah Browne
	Jada-Renee Bland
	Jamant Hanshaw
	Joline Nunes
	Kyle Gayle
	Marcel Pawlas
	Stefany Lazar
	Tierra Monét
	Trevor Swain
	Yun Gao

First edition of 800 copies, 2018
Printed in Sweden by Göteborgstryckeriet
Copyright © 2018 Eytys AB, All rights reserved

ISBN 978-91-982621-6-2

Eytys AB, Tegnérlunden 3, 111 61 Stockholm, Sweden
EYTYS.COM